Aristophanes

The Acharnians of Aristophanes

Aristophanes

The Acharnians of Aristophanes

ISBN/EAN: 9783337005450

Printed in Europe, USA, Canada, Australia, Japan

Cover: Foto ©Thomas Meinert / pixelio.de

More available books at **www.hansebooks.com**

DUBLIN UNIVERSITY PRESS SERIES

THE

ACHARNIANS· OF ARISTOPHANES

TRANSLATED INTO

ENGLISH VERSE

BY

ROBERT YELVERTON TYRRELL

M A DUBLIN   D LIT Q UNIV

:LLOW OF TRINITY COLLEGE DUBLIN AND REGIUS PROFESSOR OF GREEK

DUBLIN: HODGES FIGGIS & CO. GRAFTON-STREET

ONDON: LONGMANS GREEN & CO. PATERNOSTER-ROW

1883

DUBLIN:

PRINTED AT THE UNIVERSITY PRESS,

BY PONSONBY AND WELDRICK.

PREFACE.

IT will be asked, why should there be another translation of the *Acharnians*? Have we not versions
by Mitchell, Frere, Walsh? And what improvement
does the translator think he can make on their efforts?
I answer, I have not essayed the same task as these
learned and ingenious gentlemen. I have not aimed
at the same mark. I have sought to produce a
metrical version of the *Acharnians* which shall be
practically as literal as a prose version. Lecturing
during last Trinity Term (1882) on the *Acharnians* I
found that explanation was so closely intertwined
with translation that it was expedient to write out a
version of the play to be used with my class. I found
that it was nearly as easy to metrify the unrhymed
portions as to translate them into prose which should
at all adequately represent the manner of the original. Unrhymed lyric metres are, I think, unsuited to
comedy, whatever view may be held about their fit-
ness to convey to English readers a due impression
of the effect of a tragic choral ode. I was, therefore,
bound to essay rhyme. In the rhymed parts the ver-

A 2

sion will, of course, be found not to be so literal as in the unrhymed. But even with the shackles of rhyme my version will be seen to be very much closer to the original than those of Mitchell, Frere, or Walsh, who sometimes appear to me to make the Greek little more than a peg on which to hang poems of their own. I have tried never to omit a thought contained in the Greek (except in the interests of that reticence on certain topics which modern refinement demands), and I have never imported a new thought to obtain a rhyme, or for any purpose except to elucidate the sense.

If, in thus literally presenting the play in an English garb, I have given some help to learners, then I have succeeded to some extent. But if I have, in so doing, lost the life and spirit of the original, then I have signally failed. I hope my translation is less unsuggestive of Aristophanes than the versions above mentioned. The versifier, however accomplished, who allows his fancy to stray from the text before him, may show much cleverness, and achieve many excellent effects; but he often fails to achieve that effect which is most of all desirable, the reproduction of something like the tone and manner of his original. My version, as I have said, was undertaken with the practical design of making it serve as a running commentary on the text. But I have not tried to enable the student to dispense with an annotated edition of the play. I could have hardly done that without reprinting the Greek text. Moreover, there are cheap and excellent editions of the *Acharnians* (for instance, Mr. Paley's, Cambridge, Deighton, Bell & Co., 1876) which completely explain the allusions and elucidate the syntax. My notes are very few, occurring only when my own version needs explanation, or when I have translated a reading not to be found in the ordinary texts.

The puns I have usually indicated by italics. Most of the renderings of these are traditional. When I have consciously borrowed some translator's *equivoque*, I have acknowledged my debt in a note. But in what I call the traditional renderings I have not thought it necessary to investigate who first devised each, and to express my acknowledgment to him. The translation is designed mainly to meet the needs of students, who will be glad to find suggested to them a method of reproducing a play on words, but do not care who originated it. I do not claim any of them as my own, though, perhaps, some of them are.

In those whimsical substitutions of one word for another in which Aristophanes is far more laughter-moving than in his plays on words—in cases of παρὰ προσδοκίαν, as the Scholiasts call them—I think the best way to make the same effect in English is to introduce the two words, the expected and the unexpected, in the form of a correction. Thus, when Aristophanes says of Chaeris in the sixteenth verse of this play,

ὅτε δὴ παρέκυψε Χαῖρις ἐπὶ τὸν ὄρθιον,

the expression expected was παρῆλθε. To bring out

this point I have rendered, at the risk of being charged with undue expansion,

> When Chaeris in the Orthian song *appear'd*,
> Or rather *peer'd* out from behind the scene.

So again in verse 1026, Dercetes of Phyle in bewailing the steers which he has lost, says,

> καὶ ταῦτα μέντοι νὴ Δί᾽ ὥπερ μ᾽ ἐτρεφέτην
> ἐν πᾶσι βολίτοις.

Now some such word as ἀγαθοῖς is here the expected term instead of βολίτοις. But the same effect is not secured in English, as I think, unless both the expected and the unexpected word are employed,

> That kept me too, God knows, in every muck,
> No—luck, I mean.

This play abounds in admirable travesties, for the most part of Euripides, and especially of one of his plays, the *Telephus*. These I have indicated by "double inverted commas," reserving the 'single inverted commas' for other cases in which that typographical device is needed. When Aristophanes uses a phrase or verse intended to suggest a phrase or verse of Euripides, I have rendered it, when I could, by a quotation from Shakspeare or some other English poet. Thus best, perhaps, is produced in English the effect of the Greek, a sense of incongruity between the tragic passage and the comic context.

In places which conflict with our notions of delicacy, I have assumed some latitude, sometimes even introducing a different thought. This will be noticed in my rendering of the Phallic Hymn, the antistrophe of the choral ode beginning at verse 987, and the closing lyrical scene between Dicaeopolis and Lamachus. Twenty-nine verses, 775–804, I have omitted, as not being susceptible of such a treatment as I have applied to these passages.

In the lyrical parts of the play I have used the metres which seemed to me most analogous to the Greek. Sometimes it was possible to employ the very same metre as the original. I have accordingly used for the trochaic septenarius the measure of Locksley Hall,[1] save where the same is mixed with other metres, in which case I thought it better to make the versification uniform in English. For cretics, which abound in the choral odes, I have used mostly a dactylic rhythm with triple rhymes. The dochmiacs I have endeavoured to reproduce by the stanza which Mr. Swinburne has consecrated in *Atalanta*, and Bret Harte has profaned in the *Heathen Chinee*. There is a lightness combined with impressiveness in this

---

[1] Mr. Tennyson's usually perfect ear for rhythm has played him false twice in this noble poem. The diaeresis after the fifth foot is quite alien to the trochaic rhythm. It occurs twice in Locksley Hall, in

> Many a night from yonder ivied casement, | ere I went to rest,

and in

> Breadths of tropic shade and palms in cluster, | knots of Paradise.

rhythm which seems to me to suggest it as a fit vehicle for the Greek dochmiac.

Mr. Billson's clever and spirited translation of the *Acharnians*[1] reached my hands last midsummer, after my own version had been completed. His design is altogether different from mine; and I cannot help thinking that the attempt to render the iambic trimeters as well as the lyrical measures in rhyme imposes on the translator, however ingenious, insuperable difficulties. It is at all events quite inconsistent with my aim, which is to make a literal translation. Moreover, it seems to me that the rhyme in the parts of the play which are written in iambic trimeters actually injures the effect, and suggests rather a pantomime or a burlesque than a polished composition.

I find that my emendation of verse 1093 has been in part anticipated in Bergk's new edition of the Greek lyric poets, which I have just seen. But his conjecture presupposes a much greater corruption of the MSS. than mine.

---

[1] London: Kegan Paul, Trench & Co., 1882.

INTRODUCTION.

A PLAY of Aristophanes is, as a whole, like nothing else in ancient or modern literature. In fact, we have no name for it. To speak of it as a comedy is to call up a multitude of associations absolutely alien to Aristophanes—intrigue, repartee, character-painting, social vignettes—and to suggest a number of names which have little more in common with him than Aeschylus has—Terence, Molière, Congreve, Sheridan. Yet farces, extravaganzas, burlesques, they were not. Such forms of dramatic effort do not deal in delicate literary criticism and unrivalled parody. Indeed, the farcical element in the plays of Aristophanes is, to us at least, their weakest part. The puns of Aristophanes are perhaps worse than the puns of Plautus. Germany calls certain forms of dramatic art *Lustspiele;* but is this felt to be quite adequate, when we come on a burst of lyric melody as sweet as Shelley and as simple as Catullus ? In seeking for something to which to liken Aristophanes, we can only say that had the 'Tempest' and the 'Midsummer Night's Dream' never been written, his work would have been even more literally incomparable than it is. Ariel and Oberon might have breathed the air which Aristophanes filled with the 'sweet jargoning' of his Birds. His works are not only plays of fancy; they are (as Mr. Symonds vigorously writes) 'debauches of the reason and imagination'; each is 'a sacrifice on the thymelé of that Bacchus who was sire, by Aphrodite, of Priapus.' It is a pity that the term τρυγῳδία, which he often uses himself to describe his dramas,[1] has not found its way into our tongue. It is a word which in itself suggests the Bacchic worship, to which we owe Greek Tragedy and Comedy alike, and is free from the associations which the name Comedy has taken on.

The *Acharnians* is the oldest of the extant plays of Aristophanes. We meet in it the earliest specimen of Greek literary criticism. Moreover, it contains one of the old Phallic hymns. Thus, curiously, the oldest comedy extant preserves the very nucleus from which comedy took her rudest beginnings. It gained the first prize, Cratinus being second, and Eupolis third. This would seem to show that literary excellence alone could secure success for a play in the time of Aristophanes. For surely the teaching of Dicaeopolis cannot have been popular at Athens in the year 425.

J. H. Frere, in a review of Mitchell's 'Aristophanes,' published in the *Quarterly Review*, vol. xxiii., p. 474, gives a

---

[1] For instance, in verses 499, 500, 628 of this play.

very clever sketch of the possible genesis of these strange creations of the genius of the Athenian poet :—

> In this species of composition the utter extravagance and impossibility of the supposed action is an indispensable requisite ; the portion of truth and reality which is admitted as a counterpoise, consists wholly in the character and language. It is a grave, humorous, impossible, GREAT LIE, related with an accurate mimicry of the language and manner of the persons introduced, and great exactness of circumstance in the inferior details. In its simple state it appears to be one of the commonest and most spontaneous products of the human mind, and usually arises in some strong expression which, a moment after, is taken literally, converted into a reality, and invested with all the circumstances of action and dialogue. We shall show that the plays now before us are capable of being traced to the kind of conversation out of which, in all probability, they did originate.

In pursuance of his ingenious theory he thus traces the origin of the *Acharnians:—*

> Let us suppose an honest, warm-tempered man, obliged (as many were at the time), like Dicaeopolis in this play, to abandon his landed property to destruction, and to take refuge in the town. We may suppose he would be likely to express his feelings nearly in this way :—

> 'If our great politicians, and your leading people here in Athens, choose to waste the public treasure in embassies and expeditions, that is their own affair ; but I do not see what right they have to bring down a Peloponnesian army to drive me out of my farm—there is no quarrel that we, country people, ever had with them to my knowledge— we should all be glad enough to let-alone for let-alone—for my part, if these enemies of our's (as they call them) would allow me to live on my farm, and buy and sell as I used to do, I'd give 'em up all the money I'm worth, and thank 'em into the bargain—and I'd go there to-morrow ;—but as for our statesmen, I'm persuaded if a Deity were to come down from heaven on purpose to propose a Peace to them, they would never listen to him.'

We have here a natural and passionate form of expression which, uttered in the hearing of a poet such as Aristophanes, was sufficient to suggest the plot of the *Acharnians* and the scene of the Demigod Amphitheüs; the rest of the play, with all its wild and fanciful circumstances, being in fact nothing more than a whimsical exemplification of the first supposition : namely, that a private citizen had succeeded in concluding and maintaining a separate peace.

The reader can now follow the details of the plot, which certainly seems to lend itself to some such theory of its evolution.

Dicaeopolis, the typical Honest Man—as opposed to the place-hunters, envoys, generals, and commissioners, who found their account in the continuance of the war—has been obliged to leave his farm, and to come up to town. But the town is hateful to him, and he is home-sick for his farm. However, he has risen early to secure a good place in the Agora, whence he may bawl down all the speakers who are not for peace. The Prytanes are late, as usual. When they arrive at high noontide, lo ! the hyberbole of Dicaeopolis bids fair to be made a reality. A Demigod presents himself before the Agora ; but, even as his cynical musing had warned the honest farmer, the Demigod Amphitheüs is flouted, and narrowly escapes arrest. Then enter characters more congenial to the Agora, and altogether hateful to Dicaeopolis. These are Commissioners from the court of Persia, who tell the delighted mob how they had spent many years and much gold in dancing attendance on the Great King, and how they have brought back with them an emissary accredited from the Persian Shah, Pseudartabas, or the Sham of Persia. This officer, the King's Eye by title, cannot speak Greek; but the Commissioners interpret his jargon as promises of money from Persia. Dicaeopolis in vain seeks to expose the imposture. The King's Eye is invited to a public banquet. Dicaeopolis is now driven to desperation. He calls Amphitheüs, and giving him eight drachmas, bids him go at once to Sparta, and conclude a private peace for himself, his family, and good woman.

During the absence of Amphitheüs, Dicaeopolis is further incensed by the arrival of an Envoy from the King of Thrace, whose auxiliary cohort of Odomantians steal the farmer's luncheon. Dicaeopolis dissolves the assembly by announcing unfavourable omens in the sky. Amphitheüs comes back to him with various samples of Peace, and the sample labelled 'Thirty years by land and sea' is accepted with much satisfaction. Amphitheüs retires, fearing lest he should again encounter the doughty burghers of Acharnae, who had pursued him in wrath for daring to carry samples of Peace with hated Sparta.

These Acharnians (who compose the Chorus) now come on the stage, hot with running and with indignation. They are at first for stoning Dicaeopolis, the peace-buyer; but he at last persuades them to let him plead his cause; and, after a visit to Euripides, from whom he borrows a select assortment of the rags used in his principal tragedies, wherewith to excite the compassion of the Chorus, he makes such a clever defence of the Spartans (for whom, however, he professes hearty abhorrence) that he enlists the sympathies of half the Chorus in his favour. The rest invoke the warlike Lamachus. But Dicaeopolis withstands him to the face, and proclaims free trade with Peloponnesus.

After the Chorus have sung the Parabasis, the effects of the act of Dicaeopolis begin to appear. A Megarian enters, who is very glad to dispose of his two daughters (whom he has disguised as sows, thus giving an occasion for much clever but coarse banter) for a hank of onions and a peck of salt. But the delight of the Megarian at having disposed of his family so profitably is rudely checked by an Informer, who threatens to denounce him for importing contraband goods. Dicaeopolis expels the Informer by means of his Market Clerks, three Stout Thongs from Flayborough, and the Chorus congratulate him on the comforts which he is enjoying. Then enters a Boeotian with wares of various kinds, chiefly poultry, for sale. He agrees finally to exchange his goods for some peculiarly Attic produce. Just then appears Nicarchus, an Informer. This is most opportune. What more peculiarly Attic product than an Informer ? Nicarchus is at once seized and packed like crockery on the shoulders of the Boeotian. He conveys away the Informer, who is pursued by the jeers of Dicaeopolis and the Chorus.

The Chorus sing a pretty ode in denunciation of War and in praise of Peace, whom the Coryphaeus woos in song as the bride of his hopes. The rest of the play is devoted to the painting of scenes in which the comforts and pleasures of Dicaeopolis are sharply contrasted with the sufferings of Lamachus and other victims of the War; while the Chorus, now altogether converted to sympathy with Dicaeopolis, are eager to congratulate the happy possessor of eight drachmas'-worth of Peace, and to celebrate his attainment of the prize wineskin, which he bears in triumph from the stage.

Characters in the Play.

DICAEOPOLIS, *an Athenian Farmer.*

Herald.

AMPHITHEÜS.

Commissioner, returned from Persia.

PSEUDARTABAS, *or* The Sham of Persia.

Envoy, returned from Thrace.

Chorus of Old Acharnians.

CEPHISOPHON.

EURIPIDES.

LAMACHUS.

A Megarian.

Two Daughters of the Megarian.

An Informer.

A Boeotian.

NICARCHUS, *an Informer.*

Servant of Lamachus.

Peasant.

Bridesman.

Messenger.

THE ACHARNIANS

OF

ARISTOPHANES.

SCENE—*The Pnyx at Athens.*

DICAEOPOLIS, *alone.*

[*Moralises on his theatrical experiences.*]

Dic. How oft have I been vex'd to the very soul!
How seldom had a treat! A brace, perhaps;
Two brace, at most—and then my disappointments—
Oh, they were millions, billions—sea-sand-illions.
Come then : What did I really enjoy ? .
Yes : one sight fill'd my soul with delectation,
Cleon disgorging those five talents. Ah,
How I enjoy'd it! How I love the Knights
Still for that deed, "one worthy Hellas' thanks."
But then, *per contra* stands that stage surprise
Most shocking, when I sat with mouth agape
Waiting for Aeschylus, and the crier call'd—
'Theognis, bring your chorus on'; just fancy
The shock it gave me. Well, my second treat
Was when Dexitheüs, after Moschus, came
To sing 'Bœotia.' Then this very year

I nearly died, and got a squint withal,
When Chaeris in the Orthian song *appear'd,*
Or rather *peer'd* out from behind the scene.
But never did I feel so keen a smart—
Not from the time when I began to wash,
And feel the soapsuds in mine eyes—as now,
To find the Pnyx deserted on the day,
The regular day, fix'd for a morning meeting.
There are the people in the *Agora*
Chatting in knots, and running here and there,
To shun the ruddled rope; the Prytanes
Not yet arrived : they soon will pour in late,
Pushing and jostling for the highest step,
Down the steep bank in crowds—you'd scarce believe it.
Yet for the Peace they care not—" O my country ! "—
But as for me, I take my constant way
The very first to the Pnyx, and take my seat ;
And finding no one there, I grunt and gape,
And stretch myself, and wonder what I'll do—
Make notes, and pull my whiskers, and do sums,
And turn my eyes to the fields most wistfully;
In love with Peace, disgusted with the town,
Homesick for my own ward, which ne'er would say—
' Go buy your charcoal, dinner-wine, or oil.'
It knew not ' buy' : bore everything itself :
And that most grating *buy-word* was unheard.
So now I'm here to-day, downright resolved
To shout, and bawl, and rail at every speech
That touches any question but the Peace.
Here come the Prytanes, at high noontide !
Said I not so ?   The very thing I told you !—
Pushing and jostling for the foremost place !

Enter Prytanes, Herald, AMPHITHEÜS, *and* Citizens.

Herald. Pass on to the front; pass on, and be within
The sacred circle.
Amph.   Is the question put?
Herald. Has anyone a motion?
Amph.   *I* have.
Herald.   Who?
Amph. Amphitheüs!
Herald.   What! No son of man?
Amph. (*parodying the genealogical Prologues of Euripides*)
                                        No, no.
I am a god. " Son of Triptolemus   ·
And Ceres was Amphitheüs; and his son
Was Celeüs, mate of Phaenarete
My grandam; thence Lycinus, and from him
Am I, a god:" and charter'd by the gods
Alone to make a truce with Lacedaemon.
But, tho' a god, no travelling-allowance
Have I ; the authorities wont give the order.
Herald. Police!
Amph. (*as he is being dragged away*).   Triptolemus and
    Celeüs,
Ye will not see me wrong'd.
Dic.   Right Honourables,
Ye wrong this House in seeking to arrest
My friend for striving to make peace, and so
" Hang up your bruisèd shields for monuments."   ·
Herald. Silence! Sit down!
· *Dic.*   No, by my fay, unless
You put forthwith the question of the Peace.
Herald. The Envoys from the Shah!

                    B 2

Dic.   The Shah, indeed ! [1]
I'm sick of Envoys, peacocks, and such humbug.
  Herald. Silence !
  Dic.   Hullo ! My—Susa, what a figure !
  Commissioner. You sent us, gentlemen, to Persia's King
(Drawing twọ drachmas as our pay *per diem*),
Euthymenes being Archon.
  Dic.   Ah, those drachmas !
  Com. And we *did* suffer on our journey thro'
Caÿster's plains—in curtain'd palanquins,
Luxuriously bestow'd on cushions soft—
Poor wretches that we were !
  Dic.   And I, of course,
Was blest beyond compare—bestow'd on straw
Hard by the rampart.
  Com.   Then, as we were guests,
We *had* to drink, neat too, from gold and crystal,
Their excellent wines.
  Dic.   O city ' stern and wild,'
What game these High Commissioners make of you !
  Com. Yes, Orientals estimate their heroes
By their capacity for food and drink.
  Dic. And we by other-guess sorts of aptitudes !
  Com. So in four years we reach'd the royal palace ;
But found the King had gone to keep an easement.
And then he was engaged on the Hills of Gold
Eight months.
  Dic.   And in what timĕ did he despatch
His business ?

---

  [1] 62. This is not to be translated, ' what king.'   The absence of the
article shows that the king of Persia is meant.   Cf. for use of *ποῖος*, 109,
157, 761.

Com.   On the day of the full moon.
Then he return'd; then entertain'd his guests,
And served us up baked beef: yes, beeves baked whole.
  Dic. Who ever heard of beeves baked whole; what rubbish!
  Com. Yes, and a chicken thrice as big as that
Great chicken, Cleonym. 'Twas called—a gull.
  Dic. Thus did you *gull* us out of those two drachmas.
  Com. And now we've brought with us a Persian—*sham*,
The Eye of the Shah.

Enter PSEUDARTABAS, *the* SHAM OF PERSIA, *with a mask
representing one great eye.*

Dic.   I would a crow would peck
That same eye out; ay, and yours, too, Sir Envoy.
  Herald. The Eye of the Shah!
  Dic.   O good Lord Heracles,
In Heaven's name, friend, is your eye a porthole?
Or do you keep a lookout for the dockyard,
Rounding the point? Is that a porthole flap
That hangs below it? (*Pointing to his beard.*)
  Com.   Come then, Persian Sham,
And tell the message of the Shah to Athens.
  Ps. iartaman exarxas apissonasatra.
  Com. You catch his meaning, friends.
  Dic.   Not I, i'faith.
  Com. He says the Shah intends to send you gold;
Speak up and let them clearly hear you—gold.
  Ps. None money, Greeky bahnchoot, *no get* gold.
  Dic. Ah, me! It's all too plain.
  Com.   What does he say?

Dic. 'What,' do you ask ?   He says we'll ' *no get* gold.'
We're fools to look for money from the East.
   Com. No, no.   The word was *nuggets*, gold in nuggets.
   Dic. Nuggets ?   Well, you're a diplomate.   Meantime,
· Withdraw.   I would cross-question him apart.
Now, sir—and keep your eye upon this strap—
Tell me the truth, or else I'll dye you red
As dye of Sardis—did the Shah send gold ?

                              [*He shakes his head.*

Then we have been just hoodwink'd by our envoys ?

                              [*He nods assent.*

These fellows nod Greek, tho' they know it not,
They 're of this very town, I'm sure.   That Eunuch·
Is Cleisthenes, son of Sibyrtias.
" O thou, confess'd of most aspiring"—stern,[1]
Is it with such a beard thou com'st before us,
Dress'd as an Eunuch ?   Who's the other one ?
Doubtless the beardless Straton.
   Herald.   Silence ; seats !
The Senate summoneth the Great King's Eye
To the town mess.
   Dic.   Ah, this is worse than hanging.
Here I must cool my heels, while every door
Flies open to receive the diplomates.
Well ! I will do a deed of dreadful note :
Where is Amphitheüs ?
   Amph.   Here.

---

[1] 119.   I read ἐξευρημένε with the MSS.   The conj. ἐξυρημένε is ' from
the purpose ' of criticism.   The Schol. tell us that σπλάγχνον was the
word which stood in the verse of Eur. here parodied.   It was governed
no doubt by some such word as ἔχων, expressed or understood.

Dic.   Take these eight drachmas
And make a Peace with Sparta for me only,
My family and good woman.
          (*To the Prytanes*)   You, the rest
Stick to diplomacy like gaping fools.
  Herald. Stand forth, Theorus, envoy from Sitalces.
                              [*The Envoy stands forth.*
  Dic. Another humbug 's being usher'd in.
  Env. Our stay in Thrace would not have been so long—
  Dic. But that the purse that paid you was so long.
  Env. But that the whole of Thrace was under snow
And all the rivers frozen.
  Dic.   Just the time
Theognis with his frigid platitudes
Was freezing Athens.
  Env.   During that cold season
I with Sitalces was discussing—well—
Some wines of his.   Now, *there's* a man that's madly
In love with Athens.   Why, he dotes on you ;
He even used to scribble on the walls,
' My darling Athens.'   Well, his son, the late
Adopted child of Athens, poor wee chap,
Wanted to eat an Attic sausage at
The enrolment of the infant citizens ;
So begg'd papa to give his aid to Athens.
Whereon he made libation, and made oath
To send such hosts, that everyone should say
At Athens ' Wheugh, a very plague of locusts.'
  Dic. Hang me if I believe a word you say
Save as regards the locusts.
  Env.   Whereupon
He's sent us the most warlike tribe in Thrace.

Dic. So it appears !

Env.   Stand forward, Thracian troops,
Brought by the Envoy.   [*Enter the Thracians.*

Dic.   What the deuce is this ?

Env. A corps of Odomantians.

Dic.   Who ? What's this ?
Who's stripped them of their Odomantian—fig-leaves ?

Env. These will swashbuckler all Boeotia
For drachmas twain *per diem.*

Dic.   ' Drachmas twain '
To these uncircumcisèd dogs.   I' faith,
Honest Jack Tar, our country's wooden wall,
Would curse and swear ! Ah, what is this ?   Stop thief,
They have robb'd my leeks, this Odomantian corps.

Env. (*to the* Od.) Come, drop those leeks ! (*to* Dic.) You'd
        better keep your distance,
They 've got their garlic-courage like the game-cocks.

Dic. And could you look at me, Right Honourables,
A native, so abused by foreigners ?
Here ! I demand the adjournment of the house ;
The heavens frown, I feel a drop of rain.

Herald. The Thracians now will go, and come again
Tomorrow's morrow.   The debate's adjourn'd.

Dic. Ah me, I've lost my little bit of lunch.
But here's Amphitheüs come back from Sparta ;
Good day, Amphitheüs !

Amph.   No good day for me
'Till I make good my flight from these coal-heavers.

Dic. Why, what's the matter ?

Amph.   I was hastening home
Bearing these samples in my hands ; at once
Some old Acharnians got scent of them,

Close-grained, as hard as nails, old hearts of oak
And maple, veterans of Marathon.
Forthwith they raised a cry, " O beast most foul,
What mean those samples, and our vines cut down ? "
So they began to fill their pokes with stones,
And I to run, and they to give me chase
All in full cry.
  Dic.   Well, let them bawl away :
Have you the samples ?
  Amph.   Yes, faith ; three of 'em,
This is the brand ' quinquennial.'
  Dic.   Faugh !
  Amph.   Well ?
  Dic.   Bad !
It smells of turpentine and galley-rigging.
  Amph. Try the ' decennial' brand.
  Dic.   Dont like the bouquet,
It smacks too strongly of diplomacy
And shilly-shallying of our allies.
  Amph. Well here's the sample labell'd, ' Thirty years,
By land and sea.'
  Dic.   O feast of Dionysus !
There's a bouquet ! of nectar and ambrosia
And never-getting-ready-three-days'-rations !
The sample on my palate cries aloud,
' Go where you will ' ; this I accept ; of this
I make libation ; e'en the last drop of it
I'll drain, and send Acharnae to the deuce :
While I from war and trouble free will keep
The feast of Dionysus-in-the-fields.
  Amph. I 'll run away from these old *carbonari.*

Enter the Chorus of Acharnians *in pursuit of* DICAEOPOLIS, *who has left the stage.*

STROPHE.

This way, this, my friends, pursue him; ask of every passer-by
Have they seen him. We must seize him. 'Tis a duty you and I,
Every townsman, owes his country. Tell me, tell me, I demand,
Where on earth the fellow's vanish'd with the samples in his
            hand.
    He is off! He has gone! He has fled us!
      Ah, heavily age on us leans.
    He would not have easily led us
      When I was a lad in my teens,
    When I ran a dead heat with Phaÿllus,
      With my great bag of coal on my back ;
    Ah, we knew not the pace that could kill us
      In our teens when we shoulder'd the sack.

ANTISTROPHE.

But the fellow has escaped us, now that poor old Frosty-face
Feels his legs so stiff and heavy, far too heavy for a race.
But we'll chase him; never shall he laugh to find our efforts
            slack ;
Ne'er escape, with old Acharnae's doughty burghers on his
            track.
    He has dared—O ye Gods!—with the foemen
      To parley, tho' " grimvisag'd strife "
    'Twixt them and Acharnae's old yeomen
      For our hearths and our homesteads is rife.

But like a sharp stake[1] in their inwards,
    Or a rush driven home to the hilt,
I'll stick, ere the blood of my vineyards
    'Neath the foot of the foeman be spilt.
Come, I feel like *Stony Batter*:[2] found he *shall* be; and I will
Batter him with *stones*, the ruffian; pelt him till I've had my fill.
  Dic. Silence !
  Cho.   Silence all ! ye heard him ; there's the man
        we seek ; despite
All our ire, we must be patient till he's done the solemn rite.
                                    [*The* Chorus *retire.*

  Dic. Silence, silence,
Let the Maund-bearer come a little space
To the front. Let Xanthias set the phallus up :
Put down the maund. Let the first rite begin.
  Girl. O mother, hand me up the ladle here :
I want to pour the sauce upon the cake.
  Dic. There, that will do. O father Dionysus,
Be our approach to thee acceptable ;   ·
And our household's oblations ; may thy feast
Held in the fields, and far from war's array,
Bring blessing to us all ; and blest to me
Be thou my Peace called ' Thirty-years.' Come, child,
Meetly and duly take the basket up

---

  [1] 231. I read καὶ σκόλοψ ὀξύς, ὀδυνηρός, ἐπίκωπος, ἵνα, which corre-
sponds to the strophic verse 216.   The first cretic is resolved in the
strophe, and is not resolved in the antistrophe. The same phenomenon is
to be observed in the next verse, where in the last foot but one the cretic
is pure in the antistrophe and resolved in the strophe.
  [2] 234. Stony Batter is the name of a rather disreputable district in the
northern part of Dublin.

With face as prim as prunes.   How blest the man
Who thee shall wed, and get upon thee—weasels
As *piquant* as thyself at blush of dawn.
Move on, and in the crowd look out your sharpest
That no one get a nibble at your trinkets.
You, Xanthias, must hold the phallus up,
You and your boy, behind the maund-bearer,
And I'll come next and sing the phallic song ;
You, wife, do audience[1] from the wall.   Now, on !

[*The wife retires.* DICAEOPOLIS, *his* Maidservant, *and his*
       Daughter *march in procession round the stage, while*
       DICAEOPOLIS *sings the Phallic hymn.*]

O Phales, thou whom Bacchus chose
To roam with him, where'er he goes,
Mid routs and revels, belles and beaux,
       Wherever beauty charms,
At last I greet thee.   Six years now
Have fled ; and with a cheerful brow
I greet my homestead, safe enow,
       From arms and war's alarms.
'Tis sweeter far, sweet Phales, to my mind
The buxom Thracian wench to filching find,
With brushwood-laden head—and find her not unkind.
       How sweet to clasp her shapely waist !
       How sweet her honey'd lip to taste !
       Phales, come and drink with me,
       Such a cup I have for thee !

---

[1] 262. Perhaps for θεῷ we should read θείου.   It seems unnatural that
he should ask his wife to 'look on,' whereas fumigation was an essential
part of most Greek religious rites.

ERRATUM.

PAGE 28—NOTE, line 1, *for* θειοῦ *read* θείου.

With face as prim as prunes.   How blest the man
Who thee shall wed, and get upon thee—weasels
As *piquant* as thyself at blush of dawn.
Move on, and in the crowd look out your sharpest
That no one get a nibble at your trinkets.
You, Xanthias, must hold the phallus up,
You and your boy, behind the maund-bearer,
And I'll come next and sing the phallic song ;
You, wife, do audience[1] from the wall.   Now, on !

> [*The wife retires.* DICAEOPOLIS, *his* Maidservant, *and his*
> Daughter *march in procession round the stage, while*
> DICAEOPOLIS *sings the Phallic hymn.*]

O Phales, thou whom Bacchus chose
To roam with him, where'er he goes,
Mid routs and revels, belles and beaux,
    Wherever beauty charms,
At last I greet thee.   Six years now
Have fled ; and with a cheerful brow
I greet my homestead, safe enow,
    From arms and war's alarms.
'Tis sweeter far, sweet Phales, to my mind
The buxom Thracian wench to filching find,
With brushwood-laden head—and find her not unkind.
    How sweet to clasp her shapely waist !
    How sweet her honey'd lip to taste !
    Phales, come and drink with me,
    Such a cup I have for thee !

Rich with the joys that Peace can yield,
'Twill cure thee when with wine thy brain hath reel'd,
And 'mid the chimney's sparks shall hang the useless shield.

Chorus (catching sight of DICAEOPOLIS).

There he is: the very man:
Pelt him all who pelt him can.

Dic. Good gods what's the matter, you'll break the tureen.
Chorus. Nay, it 's you we are stoning: to kill you we mean.
Dic. Acharnian Aldermen, what have I done ?
Chor. Done ?   Every villainy under the Sun !
Made a peace with the foemen ; your country betray'd ;
Yet to look in our faces you are not afraid.
Dic. You don't know why I made it : just listen awhile.
Chor. Never ; soon shall these stones be your sepulchre's
       pile.
Dic. Just wait till you hear me : have patience, my friends.
Chor. No, never ; no words can for deeds make amends.
Worse than Cleon ! whom soon for his cavalier foes
I will cut up as small as the shoetops he sews.
No ! I'll hear no more speeches about the transaction :
You've made peace with Laconia ; I'll have satisfaction.
Dic. Good my friends, the Laconians just put on one side,
And then on my Peace and its blessings decide.
Chor. Its blessings ! With Spartans ? The thing is absurd ;
They've no care for their honour, their shrines, or their word.
Dic. We're hard on the Spartans, I know : all the same,
They are not for *all* of our troubles to blame.
Chor. Not for all of our troubles ? You villain, how dare
       you
Say this to my face ? And you fancy I'll spare you ?

Dic. Not for all.   All along, from the very beginning,
I could show them more sinn'd against sometimes than sin-
    ning.
Chor. Sinn'd against!   It's enough a man frantic to send.
So you venture the foes of your land to defend.
Dic. And to prove that I fancy I speak common sense,
With my head on this block I will make my defence.
Chor. But come, my friends, why are we sparing the varlet;
Come, pelt him until every inch of him's scarlet.
Dic. How this old charcoal log has flared up into flame !
Consider, now, really am I to blame ?
Chor. Never, never.
Dic.   That's hard.
Chor.   S'death, I'll listen no more.
Dic. Don't say so, good friends, now.
Chor.   Your death's at the door.
Dic. Well, it's worse for your loved ones. The biter is bit.
I have hostages from you ; their weasands I'll slit.
Chor. Why, what is he threat'ning ? What makes him so bold ?
Has he got in his clutches some lambs of our fold ?
Dic. Pelt away, as you please. Then I'll slaughter this Creel,
To see if for coal-kind you sympathy feel.
Chor. Death and ruin !   The Coal-creel, my fellow pa-
    rishioner,
Oh, spare him, nor ruin your humble petitioner.
, *Dic.* I tell you I'll kill him ; bawl on, I won't hear.
Chor. You kill me in killing the Creel I hold dear.[1]

---

[1] 336. It does not seem to have been observed that 284–301 corre-
sponds antistrophically with 335–346. The following slight corrections
then become requisite : Verses 338, 339, should run :—

ἀλλὰ νυνὶ λέγ᾽ εἰ σοὶ δοκεῖ, τόν τέ Λακε-
δαιμόνιον αὐτὸν ὅ, τι τῷ τρόπῳ σοῦ φίλον.

And in verse 345 τὸ should be omitted before βέλος.

Dic. You would not hear *me*—not five minutes ago.

Chor. Well, now we will hear; if you like, you can show
What's the ground of your liking for Sparta; speak freely.
I'll never be false to my little Coal-creelie.

Dic. You must throw down those stones ere I utter a word.

Chor. There they are on the ground; and now down with
your sword.

Dic. But take care you've got none in your cloak's ample
fold.

Chor. No. I've shaken it out; you can see it unroll'd.
But a truce to palaver. Your sword to the ground.
Why, we'll throw out the stones as we trip it around.

[*The* Chorus *dance round, shaking out the stones from
their cloaks.*

Dic. I thought you'd all give o'er your caterwauling.[1]
And, let me tell you, never nearer came
Death to brave souls of Parnes—coals, I mean—
All through these dense parishioners of theirs.
The Creel's in such a funk, it voided on me

---

[1] 347. I have translated the conjectural reading ἀνήσειν τῆς βοῆς. The
MSS. give ἀνασείειν βοήν, which may be explained as a παρὰ προσδοκίαν for
ἀνασείειν χέρας, which was a form of asking for quarter: with this reading
and explanation I would render:

> I thought you'd soon throw up the sponge—or rather,
> Give up your bawling. Never nearer came &c.

Or else, perhaps, the allusion is to the foregoing words, ἐκσέσεισται
σειόμενον, σειστός. It should then be rendered:

> So, with all your shaking, you felt bound to shake
> Before my eyes this empty show of clamour.

Or simply:

> So you were bound to make a great to-do.

Παρνήθιοι is certainly the right reading for Παρνάσσιοι.

A lot of coal-dust,[1] like a cuttle-fish.
'Tis strange, that in the milk of human kindness
Should be so sour a drop, that men should pelt
And hoot a man, and never let him plead
His cause, tho' temper'd fair as e'er was wine-cup.
See! I will state the whole of Sparta's case,
My head upon the block ; and yet I love
My life as well as you or any man.
> *Chor.*   The block then produce,
>   And your stand by it take,
>   And show us what use
>   Is the case you can make.

For I'm really anxious to know what you *can* find to say for
     their sake.
Therefore, since you invite the penalty
Yourself, bring forth the block, and make your plea.

Dic. Look here : you see the block ; the man stands here
Who is to speak ; there is not much of him.
Trust me, I will not "do my harness on,"
But I will say what I believe for Sparta.
And yet I'm very nervous, for I know
The boors become ecstatic if some rogue
Praise them, and laud their city up and down,
And that is how they're humbugg'd unawares.
Our worthy elders, too, I know them well ;
They care for nothing but their stinging verdicts.
I can't forget how I was served by Cleon
For last year's play : he forced me into court,

---

350. Perhaps we should read τῆς μαρίλης τὴν συχνήν. Cp. τῆς γῆς
τὴν πολλὴν, Cobet's correction of τὴν γῆν τὴν πολλὴν in Thuc. ii. 48.

And slander'd and beslobber'd me with lies,
And splutter'd like Cycloborus, and slang'd me,
So that I really felt myself half dead,
Being dragg'd, all draggled, thro' that case's mire.
So let me now, before I make my speech,
Get myself up in guise most pitiable.

Chor.   What's the reason or rhyme
                Of your tricks and your traps.
Go to Hieronyme—
        When you find him, perhaps,
You'll get one of his "heavy-plumed, shaggy-hair'd, invisibility
        caps."
So broach the arts of Sisyphus straightway:
This is a case that will not brook delay.

Dic. Now I must summon up a heart of grace,
And go and see Euripides.   Hullo!
        [*He knocks at a door*, which Cephisophon *opens.*

Ceph. Who's there.
Dic.   Pray, is Euripides at home?
Ceph. " He is, yet is not."   Catchest thou the thought?
Dic. 'At home, and not at home?'   How's that?
Ceph.   Even so.
His soul's abroad collecting versicles;
His bodily presence here play-mongering
In a garret.
    Dic.   Happy, happy, happy poet!
Whose slave can logic-chop so learnedly :
Summon him.
    Ceph.   But I could not.

c

Dic.   But you must.
I will not go away : I'll keep on knocking.
Euripides, my sweet Euripides !
Open to me, if ever you admitted
A mortal man.   I'm Dicaeopolis
Of *Chollid* ward.
 Eur.   This is no *holiday.*
 Dic. Well, bid them turn the house-front and display
Th' interior.
 Eur.   But I could not.
 Dic.   But you must.
 Eur. I'll do, then, as you ask ; but won't come down.
 Dic. Euripides !
 Eur.   What screamest ?
 Dic.   Why not write
Down here, instead of perching in that cockloft ?
That's why your characters go lame before
They come to us.   And what's the use of all
These sorry weeds and stage rags ?   That is why
You put so many beggars on the stage.
But I beseech you, for sweet pity's sake,
Give me some rag from some old worn-out play ;
For to the Chorus I am bound to make
A speech ; and if I fail, 'twill cost my life.
 Eur. Rags, and what rags?   Those in which Oeneus here
Erst played, that " very feeble fond old man " ?
 Dic. Not Oeneus, no.   There was a worse than that.
 Eur. Phoenix, blind Phoenix ?
 Dic.   No, not his ; there was
A character more ragged still than Phoenix.
 *Eur.*What " thing of shreds and patches " would'st thou have ?
Is it the beggar Philoctetes' rags ?

Eur. What, then ? The squalid tatters of the lame
Bellerophon ?

Dic.   No, lame he was indeed,
And used to beg, and well could wag his tongue.

Eur. I know the one you think of : Telephus,
The Mysian king.

Dic.   The very man.   ̖

Eur.   Here, boy!
Bring me the tattered garb of Telephus ;
It lies upon the Thyestean rags,
'Twixt them and Ino's. Take them ; there they are.

Dic. O Zeus, that lookest down on every thing,
And seëst through them all, may I succeed
In garbing me in guise most miserable.
And since you've been so kind, Euripides,
Lend me the other properties that go
Along with these : I mean the Mysian cap ;
" For I this day must play the beggar here—
Be what I am, but other far appear."
The house must recognise me as myself—
The Chorus standing by like fools, that I
At the old cocks may poke my quiddities.

Eur. Here. "Thy device is shrewd, and right thy rede."

Dic. Oh, blessings on you ; "and on Telephus—
What's in my thoughts." Bravo, I'm getting full
Of quibbles. But I want a beggar's staff.

Eur. Take, then, the staff, and leave the "marble halls."

Dic. My soul, thou seëst how I'm driven forth,
Though many properties I lack. But thou
Be in thy begging whine importunate.

(*To Euripides*) Lend me a basket that the lamp has burn'd
A hole in.

Eur.   Of this wicker thing, poor wretch,
What need hast thou ?

    Dic.   Need have I none, but want it.

    Eur. I tell you, you annoy me, and must go.

    Dic. Ah ! may God bless you—like your blessed mother.

    Eur. Now pray be off.

    Dic.   Well, give me just one thing—
A little cup with broken rim.

    Eur.   Oh, take it.
A murrain with it ! You're a bore, I tell you.

    Dic. Thou knowest not yet what mischief thou art doing.
But, sweet Euripides, just one thing more.
A pipkin with a hole in't, plugg'd with sponge.

    Eur. You're robbing me of all my tragic art.
Take it and go.

    Dic.   I will. And yet, how can I ?
One thing I need, and if I get it not
I'm ruin'd. Listen, dear Euripides ;
If I get this I'll go and come not back :—
Some refuse cabbage leaves to fill my basket.

    Eur. You'll ruin me : there !—now you've taken all
My tragic genius.

    Dic.   Well, I'll ask no more.
Indeed I am too troublesome : and I
" Bethought me not that I misliked the Lords."
Ah, me ! I'm ruin'd : I forgot the thing
On which depends the whole of my success.
Darling Euripides, upon my life,
I'll never ask you for another gift,

I'll ask this only ; only this one loan :
Do borrow me a chervil from your mother.
   Eur. He's insolent.   Ho! "close the portalice."
   Dic. My soul, we must proceed without our chervil.
Knowest thou what a deed of high emprise
Thou takest up in pleading for the Spartans ?
Forward, my soul ; this is the starting-post.
Dost hesitate ?   Advance ; for thou hast had
An adult's dose of thy Euripides—
My soul declines with thanks : come then, my heart,
' My breaking heart,' step forth, and lay thine head
Upon the block : when thou hast said thy say
Fear nothing.   Forward ! March ! Bravo, my heart !

   Chor.   How *will* it all end ?
          You're as stout as a stock,
        I tell you, my friend,
          And as firm as a rock,
To venture in sight of your country to lay down your head on
    the block,
         To meet the conviction
          Of everyone here
        With flat contradiction !
         The man has no fear !
Very well, since you will have it so, say on, my fine fellow
    I'll hear.

   Dic. Gentles, I pray you, be not wroth with me—
If I, a beggarman, amongst Athenians
Talk politics in this my comedy.
' Fair 's fair ' as even comedy will own,
And I will say words fair, though far from smooth.

Now Cleon cannot bring his slanderous charge
That I defame the state, with strangers present ;
For we are by ourselves ; the festival
The wine-press feast ; and so the foreigners
Are not here yet, with tributes and contingents ;
But we are by ourselves—grain husk'd and shell'd[1]—
(The Aliens being the chaff that's with the grain).
Now I abhor the Spartans heartily.
I would the God that rules o'er Taenarus
Would hurl their houses down upon them all
With earthquakes.   *My* vines, too, have felt their knives ;
And yet, my friends (for we are all friends here),
Why should we on the Spartans lay the blame ?
Certain of us—I do not say the state—
Bear that in mind—some pettifogging rascals,
Vile raps, ill-stamp'd, base, clipp'd, and counterfeit,
Vexatious informations laid against
Poor Megara's little trade in woollen cloaks ;
And if they chanced to see a water melon,
Lev'ret, or sucking pig, or head of garlic,
Or lump of salt, at once 'twas 'contraband,
Megarian goods,' and confiscated straight.
All this, I will allow, was no great thing—
The custom of the country.   Then some youths,
Rising from wine and Kottabos half mad,
A girl of Megara, Simaetha hight,
Feloniously abducted ; smarting, then,
As 'twere with blister of their native leek,
The men of Megara in reprisal stole
Two of Aspasia's girls ; thus war broke out

----

[1] The ξένοι would be the straw.

Over all Hellas through three bona robas.
Then the Olympian Pericles, in wrath,
Fulmined o'er Greece, and set her in a broil
With statutes worded like a drinking catch :
    No Megarian on land
    Nor in market shall stand
    Nor sail on the sea, nor set foot on the strand.[1]
Then the Megarians, as they starved by inches,
Begg'd Sparta to induce us to rescind
The statute made anent the bona robas ;
But, spite of Sparta's asking, we refused ;
Then Sparta's shields came rattling from their pegs.
" Then were they wrong," you'll say with Telephus:
But tell me what they should have done.   Suppose
A Spartan took a boat, and publicly
Sold, after information duly laid,
A puppy of Seriphus, would ye then
Have " sat at home at ease " ? Far from it : no,
Ye would have straightway launch'd three hundred galleys :
The town had been one scene of shouting tars,
Din round the paymaster, and noisy issue
Of the men's pay, gilding of statuettes
Of Pallas, rations measured out, piazzas
Groaning 'neath struggling crowds, and everywhere
Wineskins, oar-loops, and purchasers of jars ;
Nothing but garlic, olives, nets of leeks,
Garlands, sprats, figurantes, and black eyes ;
And what a sight the dockyard would have been,
Spars getting shaped to blades, the wooden thud
Of driven pegs, the rowlocking of oars,

---

[1] I have borrowed Mr. Paley's clever rendering here.

The boatswain's whistle, flourishes and calls :—
This you'd have done.   "And think we Telephus
Would not.   Then is our wisdom foolishness."
   Semi-Chor. 1°. What, O most foul of knaves, is't thus,
      a beggar,
You speak to us, and twit us with the chance
That here and there there might have been informers.
   Semi-Chor. 2°. Yes, and in everything he says, perdy,
He says what's fair, and not a lie in it.
   Semi-Chor. 1°. And is that any reason *he* should say it ?
But he will find his boldness cost him dear.
   Semi-Chor. 2°. Whither away ? Nay, stop. For if you strike
The man, you'll find you'll soon be hoist yourself.

   [*A struggle begins between the two* Semi-Choruses.
      Semi-Chorus 1° *being worsted, invokes the aid of*
      LAMACHUS.

Semi-Chor. 1°. Lamachus, of lightning glance,
            Hero of the Gorgon crest,
         Friend and tribesman, come, advance,
            Turn thine ear to our behest.

         Any man of war that's near
            Promptly to my succour haste—
         Captain, colonel, engineer—
            For they've gripp'd me round the waist.

   Lam. Whence comes the martial summons to the rescue ?
Where must I lend my aid, and panic spread ?
Who's roused the Gorgon from my buckler's case ?
   Dic. Ye Gods ! What plumes and what a plump of spears !
   Semi-Chor. 2°. 'Tis he has roused the Gorgon, Lamachus,
      Our city he's been sland'ring all the day.

Lam. Ha! waggest thou thy tongue so boldly, beggar?
Dic. O martial Lamachus, have mercy on me,
For that, a beggar born, I wagg'd my tongue.
Lam. What said'st thou of us? Say.
Dic.   I can't remember;
Your dreadful armour makes me giddy; pray,
Pray put away that awful—bugaboo. (*Pointing to his shield.*)
Lam. There.
Dic.   And now set it upside down for me.
Lam. 'Tis done.
Dic.   Now take the plume from out the casque.
Lam. There is a feather of it.
Dic.   Now, then, hold
My head: I'm sick: the crest has raised my gorge.
Lam. What? Puttest thou the plume to such base use?
Dic. Plume? Pray what bird's. Is it a puffinstrutter's?
Lam. Thou'lt die the death.
Dic.   Say not so, Lamachus;
I am not worthy of thy steel; thou'rt strong;
Canst do thy pleasure, being well equipp'd.
Lam. Speakest thou thus, thou beggar, to thy captain?
Dic. Am I a beggar?
Lam.   Well, what art thou?
Dic.   What?
An honest man, no Mr. Placehunter,
And since the war broke out, plain Private Trudge;
But you, Sir Fullpay Generalissimo.
Lam. I was elected.
Dic.   By a couple o' cuckoos:
And that is why I made the peace, being sick
Of seeing grey-hair'd veterans in the ranks,
And lads like you promoted to the—shirking;

Some off to Thrace, drawing three drachmas pay,
Dissolute-aliens,[1] Ruffian-swashbucklers;
Some off with General Favour; some in—Sodom,
Geres and Theodore and Co., those rogues
Of Diomaea's ward; to Camarina
Some, or to Gela, or to—Jericho.

   Lam. They were elected.

   Dic.   Yes, but what's the reason
Why you are somehow always under pay,
And none of these men here? Pray, Master Colley,
Wert ever on a diplomatic corps,
Tho' grey long since?[2] You see, he shakes his head.
And yet he's sober and industrious.
Pray Messrs. Cole,[3] and Carrier, and Oakheart,
Have any of you seen Ecbatana,
Or yet Chaonia? No! .'Tis Lamachus
Goes, and the scion of rich Coesyra,
Who only yesterday were so involved
In club-money and debts, that finally
' Out of the way ' was all their friends' advice,
Just as one cries *gare l'eau* when emptying slops.

   Lam. There is Democracy! Must this be borne?

   Dic. No : unless Lamachus is under pay.

   Lam. Well, then, on Pelops' isle I war proclaim,
And everywhere I'll harass it every way
By sea and land, with all my might and main.

---

[1] These are types of Athenian character of which we know nothing except what the Scholiasts tell us. I have embodied in my version the views of the Scholiasts.

[2] 610. I read ἔνῃ = 'last year '; ὤν is the imperfect participle.

[3] 612. For τί δαὶ Δράκυλλος I read τί δ' 'Ανθράκυλλος with Reiske. All the names should have reference to the charcoal-burning trade.

Dic. *I* to the whole of Pelops' isle proclaim
To Megara and all Boeotia
Free trade with me—but not with Lamachus.

[*Chorus come forward and sing the* Parabasis.

ANAPAESTS *or* PARABASIS *proper.*

He's right about making the Peace, and he's bringing the
    populace round.
And now for a fling at our Anapaests. Cast we our cloaks on
    the ground.
From the time when our poet first made in the playwright's
    profession a start,
He never was used to come forward to boast of his marvellous
    art ;
But now that malicious detractors are trying a notion to
    raise
That he slanders his country, and runs the Democracy down
    in his plays,   .
He thinks it is best to put in his demurrer at once, as he
    finds
That you're equally ready to change, and hasty to make up,
    your minds.
He says that he's made you his debtors by teaching you not
    to be gull'd
By the soft words that foreigners give you, nor into security
    lull'd
By swallowing doses of bunkum.   Time was when the whole
    of the town
Was led by the nose if one spouted the praise of her ' violet
    crown,'

And the moment a diplomate air'd that expression of mystical
     might,
'The crown' did the business: you scarcely could sit on
     your seats for delight.
If some flatterer said 'land of oil' there was nought you'd
     refuse him, I ween,
Tho' he gave you a title more fit for the praise of a potted
     sardine.
And that's how he's made you his debtors—by turning the
     eyes of your mind
To the rights and the wrongs of your subjects. And that is
     the reason, you'll find,
Why the envoys that come with the tribute so long to behold
     the brave poet
Who dared to tell Athens the truth when he thought it was
     right she should know it.
You may judge that the fame of his boldness has pretty well
     gone round the globe
By the two questions put by the Shah, when he sought
     Lacedaemon to probe ;
For he first asked, which side of the two the sea with her
     navy could hold,
And then he ask'd which had the bard who was given so
     freely to scold ;
For the state that had such an adviser, he said, would be
     stronger by far,
And would certainly bring by his aid to a glorious issue the
     war.
And that is why Sparta so gladly conditions of peace would
     afford,
And not be so hard about terms, if Aegina were only
     restored.

And it's not that they care for the isle; but the poet they're
    eager to rob of it;
But let him go on with his work; you'll find that he'll make
    a good job of it.
He says he'll ensure your success, and declares that, whate'er
    is the matter, he
Will give you the best of advice without any favour or
    flattery;
And never the words of deceit will you hear, or appeals to
    venality,
Or gush of unprincipled praise, but the highest and best of
    morality.

MACRON *or* PNIGOS.

(Pronounced by the actor in one breath).

Then may Cleon let fly
All his malice, and try
Every art that he knows : all his arts I defy :
'For the right' is my cry,
Never, never shall I
Like that lecherous coward[1] my country deny.

STROPHE.

Muse of Acharnae, a glowing song bring to me.
O that thy voice were as fire,.and could spring to me !
E'en as a flame, when the heart of it sickeneth,
Leaps from the embers of oak the fan quickeneth—
Leaps round the sprats that lie ready for frying there,
While the slaves all are in energy vieing there ;

---

[1] Cleon.

Stirring the pickle with oil-bubbles beading up,
"Rich-crown'd" like Mem'ry,[1] and wheaten rolls kneading up:
Come with a strain that will suit your petitioner,
Lusty but plain, to your fellow-parishioner.

EPIRRHEMA.

We old fogies have a quarrel with our country; and it's this:
That we do not get the treatment which we earn'd at Salamis.
We, the men that won your battles, deem that in our dotage still
We've a right to your attention; yet you treat us very ill.
Into public suits you drag us, poor old grey-beards that we
    are,
Laughing when we're chaff'd by every callow fledgeling at the
    Bar.
We who, deaf and dumb and bother'd, simply old play'd-out
    riff-raff,
Might as well be in an earthquake if we hadn't got our staff.
Mumbling o'er some maund'ring nonsense at the dock we
    take our place,
Able scarce to see the foggy outlines of the misty case;
But the plaintiff, making sure his Bar is vigorous and young,
Raps us smartly o'er the knuckles, phrases rolling off his
    tongue;
Has us up to cross-examine, setting word-traps in our way,
Hackling, vexing, and perplexing wretched old Methuselah.
So the verdict goes against him; and the dotard leaves the
    court,
Mumbling, sighing, grumbling, crying, in his feeble senile
    sort.

---

[1] Pindar had applied the epithet λιπαράμπυξ to Memory.

As he goes he meets his crony, and complains with piteous
  whine—
'What I'd saved to buy a coffin I must spend to pay my fine.'

ANTISTROPHE.

How can you justify Athens, when daily ye
Here before justice's paraphernalia
Ruin some greyheaded old fellow-labourer,
Haply some veteran Marathon sabrer,
Who in the battlefield often was set by you,
Wiped from his manly brow toil's honest sweat by you.
Once for the city we charged and protected her;
Now *we* are charged by those spies who 've infected her.
When the Court casts us, a fine we 've to pay to it.
This is my case : what will Marpsias[1] say to it ?

ANTEPIRRHEMA.

There's Thucydides[2] bent double : is it right that such as he
Should in body-grips be struggling with that—steppe of
  Tartary,
With the glib Cephisodemus, that forensic waterspout ?
Yet my aged friend I've witnessed by that Tartar pull'd about;

---

[1] A young Athenian advocate.

[2] Thucydides, son of Melesias, was an opponent of Pericles, by whose
influence he was banished, B.C. 445. The father of Cephisodemus had
been a τοξότης, or constable, in Athens. These τοξόται were slaves
bought by the State mainly from Scythia. Hence they are often called
Σκύθαι by Aristophanes. And hence Thucydides is here said to be grappled
by a Scythian, who, by a very bold figure, is called a 'Scythian wilderness,'
or 'steppe of Tartary,' as I have rendered the phrase.

And I dash'd aside a tear of pity, and my heart was sore
For the man that is no longer, the Thucydides of yore.
Then no words from any rascal constable in all the land,
Nor from Ceres' self, by Ceres, our Thucydides would stand.
No, his very first crossbuttock ten Evathli would have floor'd,
And three thousand Tartar bowmen he'd have easily—out-
     roar'd.
Constable Cephisodemus! He would not have cared a pin;
He'd out-constable the household, son and father, kith and kin.
No! since you're resolved the old boys sometimes from their
     doze should start,
Keep the suits *in re* the elders and *in re* the young apart.
Let the aged and the toothless charge the aged; for the
     young—
Let the fast and flippant charge them—like the brat from
     Cleinias sprung.
Be it fine, or be it exile, ever should this statute hold,
That the young should sue the young ones, and the old
     should sue the old.

Dic. Thus do I set my market's boundaries :
Here all the states of Pelops' isle may trade—
Megarians and Boeotians, if they sell
Their goods to me, but not to Lamachus.
Clerks of the market these I constitute,
Chosen by lot—three thongs from Flayborough;
Within these bounds let no informer come,
Nor any other Water-tell-tail [1] wight.

---

[1] If the play is on φάσις, ' an information against contraband goods,'
and Phasis the river, one might render—

          Or any other wight from banks o' Spy.

If it is on φάσις and φασιανός, 'a pheasant,' the play may be reproduced as

I' the market-place, in view of all, I'll set
The column with our contract graved on it.

A Megarian *enters.   He speaks in the Scotch dialect.*

Meg. Gude luck to Athens' chepe, that's lo'ed so weel
By Megara.   I've greetit for ye sair,
Sae help me God o' Freends, as ye had been
My mither; puir bairns o' a puirer feyther,
Come up to get yer bannock, an' ye may.
So tak my rede into your—empty wames ;
Wad ye be selt, or stairve ?
   Daughters.   Selt, selt.
   Meg.   Just sae ;
But wha sae daft as buy ye ?   Ye wad be
Naething but downricht loss.   But I've a plan,
A guid Megarian plan.   I'se gar ye baith
Dress up as pigs, and say I'm hawkin' pigs.
Pit an thae petitoes, and play the part
O' bein' a braw soo's farrow.   O' ma conscience,
An' ye gae hame again ye'll hunger sair.[1]
Pit an these snouts, and get into the poke,
An' mind ye grunt, and ' ugh,' and make the soun'
O' haly pigs used for the Mysteries.

in the text. If it is merely a comic coinage, containing an allusion to
φάσις, one might translate—

       Or any other base Gaugerian wight.

[1] But τὰ πρᾶτα . . . τᾶς λιμῶ can hardly mean 'the extremes of hunger.'
Ahrens ingeniously conjectures—

             εἴπερ ἰξεῖτ' οἴκαδις
   ἄκρατα, πειράσεσθε κ.τ.ἑ.

                    D

An' now I'se ca' this Dicaeopolis,
An' speer whaur is he.   Wad ye buy some soos ?
  Dic. What, a Megarian ?
  Meg.   We've come to trade.
  Dic. How goes it with you there ?
  Meg.   We sit a' day
By th' inglenook, an' fast wi' ane anither.
  Dic. And feast with one another ?   Come, that's good,
If you've a piper.   Well, what else besides ?
  Meg. Sae, sae.   When I left hame a gran' committee
Were takin' counsel for the toun to find
The best and quickest gate to gang to the deil.[1]
  Dic. Thy woes will soon be over then.
  Meg.   Ou ay.
  Dic. What else at Megara ?   How is grain sold there ?
  Meg. Wi' us it's unco dear.   Dear God's nae dearer.
  Dic. Salt, then ?
  Meg.   Ye're maisters o' the saut works, too.
  Dic. Well, garlic ?
  Meg.   Garlic ?   When ye mak a raid
Into our fields, like mice, frae time to time,
Ye howk up a' the roots o't wi' a preen.[1]
  Dic. What have you, then ?
  Meg.   Soos for the Mysteries.
  Dic. 'Tis well.   Let's see them.
  Meg.   Hoot, mon, but they 're gran'.
Feel this ane, sin ye're fain.   She's fat and braw.
  Dic. What thing is this ?
  Meg. ₁   A soo.

---

[1] I have here adopted the excellent version of Walsh, whose knowledge
of the Scotch dialect often leaves the translator no choice but to follow him.

Dic.　　　　　　What say you, you there?
What breed?
　Meg.　　　　Megarian.　Isn't she a soo?
　Dic. Not to my eyes.
　Meg.　　　　　　Weel, weel! Look at her, mon.
The Infidel! He swears she is no soo.
Weel, an ye list, I'se bet a peck o' saut
She's ca'd a soo in Greece.
　　　　　　　[775–804 *are omitted.*]
　Dic.　　　　　　Figs for the pigs!
　　　　　[*Here figs are distributed among the audience.*
Now will they eat them? Wheugh! There's gobbling for
　　you.
Where were they bred? I'm sure 'twas *Munchester.*
But, see, they haven't eaten all the figs.
　Meg. Na, na; for I was fain to tak' up ane.
　Dic. I'faith, a very pretty pair of beasts.
How much for the pigs?
　Meg.　　　　　　For ane, a hank o' leeks;
For t'other, gin ye list, a peck o' saut.
　Dic. Done! Wait you here.
　Meg.　　　　　Just sae. O god o' bargains,
Gie me the luck at this same price to sell
My ain guid wife and my ain mither, too!

　　　　　　　Enter an Informer.

　Inf. Your country?
　Meg.　　　　Megara. I'm of that ilk,
A pig-dealer.
　Inf.　　　Well, I'll denounce you both,
You and your pigs, as contraband and foes.
　　　　　　　　D 2

Meg. Ah, there it is!   There is the source of a'
That gars us greet.
Inf.   Your burr will cost you dear.
Come, drop the poke.
Meg. (*to* Dicaeopolis.) My friend, I am denounced.
Dic. By whom ?   He thinks he'll throw a light, I guess,
On the subject!   Turn him out, my market clerks.
Where is your candle if you want to throw
A light on things ?
Inf.   It's only on the foe.
Dic. You'll rue it, if you don't get out of this.
Meg. They're a sair scauld at Athens, thae informers.
Dic. Don't be afraid, my friend.   Here, take the leeks
And salt, your bonnifs' price.   And now, farewell.
Meg. Fareweel ?   Na, na; we've nae guid fare at hame.
Dic. Well, may my wish on my own head recoil
If I was hasty.
Meg.   Now, ma wee boneens,
Wi'out your feyther ye maun try to eat,
Wi' a grain o' saut, your bannocks—gin ye get 'em.

Chorus (*to the* Coryphaeus).

How fortunate the fellow is!   You see his exultation,
And soon he'll reap a harvest from his novel proclamation.
        While he sits in the market-place,
        If Ctesias should show his face,
        Or any rascally informer,
        He'll leave the place a trifle warmer.

                    (*Turning to* Dicaeopolis.)

You'll have no fear lest someone else in marketing should
    best you,
Or by his filthy presence bawdy Prepis should molest you.
    Cleonymus won't jostle you.
    You'll keep your mantle clean and new.
    Hyperbolus won't stand before you,
    With sheafs of dirty writs to bore you.
The razor'd young Cratinus, too, that idle, feckless callant,
Won't meet you in the market, with his hair dress'd *à la*
    gallant—
    That Artemon,[1] who's always dozing,
    And hurries only when composing,
    From whose foul stink might be inferr'd
    His origin from St. Goatherd.[2]
No more will Pauson vex you with his impudent grimaces,
Nor the lecherous Lysistratus, his parish who disgraces ;
    Who starves and shivers constantly,
    Steep'd to the lips in misery,
    For thrice three days, the wretched loon,
    Ay, and more, too, in every moon.

A Boeotian *enters, who speaks in the dialect of the stage Irishman.*

Boeot. Bedad, it's mighty gall'd me shouldher is.
Ismenias, lay down the pennyroy'l.

---

[1] 850. Artemon was an engineer who was in the habit of being carried
about in a carriage to inspect his works, hence he was called ὁ περιφόρητος
Ἀρτέμων. This Cratinus, being as lazy as Artemon, and a very bad character, is called, by a slight change in the phrase, not περιφόρητος, but
περιπόνηρος.

[2] Walsh's rendering of the pun is here borrowed. For another pun on
the same word, see 808.

Go aisy now ; and you, the Thaban pipers,
Take up yer pipes and play—the very divil.
   Dic. Stop, with a murrain.   Off from the door, ye wasps.
Whence did they hither wing their cursed way,
These whoreson bumble-piping cubs of Chaeris ?
   Boeot. Be the hole i' me coat, I wish them all wor hang'd.
Sure they were blowin' all the way from Thabes,
Till they blew down the blossoms off me flowers.
But you'll be buyin' somethin', if you plase—
Me chickens, or me four-wing'd locustses ?
   Dic. 'Tis well, my scone-fed friend.   What have you there ?
   Boeot. Sure I've the pick of all the place intirely :
Marjoram, pennyroyal, mats, wicks, ducks,
Jackdaws and woodcocks, coots, wrens, divers——
   Dic.   Wheugh !
You're like the winter wind, that brings the birds
Of passage to our markets.
   Boeot.   Ay, and geese,
Hares, foxes, hedgehogs, weasels, rabbits, cats,
Otters, Copaïc eels.
   Dic.   O blessed one,
Thou that to mortals bear'st their best *bonne bouche,*
Let me address the eels.
   Boeot.   " Of fifty nymphs
Of Lake Copaïs, thou the eldest born "—
Come ou' o' this, now, and oblige his honour.
   Dic. Hast come to me, my dearest heart's delight,
After long years—dream of the Green Room, and
Idol of Morychus the Gastronome ?
What, ho ! bring in the brazier and the bellows:
Look, minions, at this best of eels that now
Blesseth my sight—and after six long years.

I will bring coals to greet our lady-guest.
Speak to her: lead her in: "not e'en in death
May I be parted from thee"—stew'd in beet.
 Boeot. But where'll I get the money for her, sur?
 Dic. I'll take her as a market-toll. What else
Hast got to sell?
 Boeot.   The whole o' them.   ^
 Dic.   Your price?
Or will you take our produce back with you?
 Boeot. Ay, somethin' that's in Athens, not in Thabes.
 Dic. You'll buy our sardines, then, or crockery?
 Boeot. Sure we've got *them* at home. No; but I want
Somethin' we've not, and you have plinty of.
 Dic. I know: the very thing for exportation: .
Pack an informer up like crockery.
 Boeot. By this an' that, an' I might make me fortune,
By showin' him for a mischiévious ape.
 Dic. And here's Nicarchus coming to inform.
 Boeot. What! that spalpeen?
 Dic.   But all there is of him
Is—bad.
 Nic. Who owns the goods?
 Boeot.   They're mine, bedad,
From Thabes.
 Nic. Well I declare them contraband.
 Boeot. Why what's possessed you, that you pick a quarr'l,
And rise a ruction wid me chickabiddies?
 Nic. I'll charge you too.
 Boeot.   What did I do on you?
 Nic. Well, I'll explain far these bystanders' sakes:
You are importing wicks from hostile states.

Dic. You've got a wick to throw a light upon
A dark transaction.
  Nic.   It might set the docks
In flames.
    Dic.   One wick to set the docks in flames!
    Nic. Certainly.
    Dic.   How?
    Nic.   Thus: some Boeotian wight
Might stick the wick into a water-beetle,
Light it, and send it thro' a gutter down
Into the docks, biding his time until
The wind was high.   Then, if a spark once caught
The fleet, 'twere straightway in a blaze.
    Dic.   O villain,
All through a little wick and water-beetle.

             (DICAEOPOLIS *beats the* Informer.)

  Nic. I call you all to witness.
    Dic.   Gag the knave.
Give me some straw.   I'll pack him up like delft,
To keep him from being broken in the transit.

STROPHE.

  Chor. Yes, pack him up, like glass, with care,
        On our friend's[1] shoulders bind him fair;
        The bargain's his.   He must beware
        Lest on the way he break it.

---

[1] The Boeotian who has taken the Informer, as a specimen of Attic produce, in exchange for his wares.

Dic. I'll watch. (*Beating him*) The crock rings crack'd
            and thin :
    As full of flaws without, within,
        As God and man could make it.
Chor. What use ?
Dic.   Oh, every use.   A cup
        Of woes—a mortar to bray up
        All sorts of litigation—
        A lamp to throw official glare
        On pow'r—a mixer to prepare
        Official botheration.

                ANTISTROPHE.

Chor.   In using it, I'm very sure,
            A man could never feel secure,
            Nor ever in his house endure
                Its broken, jangling clatter.
Dic.   You'll find it strong.   Just hang the loun,
            Like empty wine-jar, upside down.
                That crock you'll never shatter.
Chor. (*to* Boeotian).
            My friend, your bargain's now secure.
Boeot.   Well, now I think I'll make for sure
                His price, and something over.
Chor.   Then take him off, and fling the cur
            On some dungheap,[1] or—filthier—
                On some accurs'd Approver.

---

[1] A phrase for getting rid of a worthless thing. I have followed the
explanation of the Scholiast, who says that συκοφάντην is used unex-
pectedly for σωρόν. *To throw a thing on any heap* was a phrase which

Dic. 'Twas a hard job to pack the rascal tight.
Now take your crockery and go your way.
Boeot. Ismenias, you spalpeen, stoop your shouldher.
Dic. Be sure you carry him securely home.
You'll have a rotten burden ; but no matter.
And if you sell him well, your fortune's made:
So far as the supply of them 's concern'd.

Enter Servant *of* LAMACHUS.

Serv. (to DIC.) Good sir !
Dic.   What is it ?   Are you calling me ?
Serv. ' What ' ?   Lamachus desires you'll let him have
A drachma's worth of thrushes for ' The Flasks,'
And for three drachmas a Copaic eel.
Dic. Who is this Lamachus that wants the eel ?
Serv. Why, Lamachus the dread, the staunch : of shield
Grogonean, and three nodding, shaggy plumes.
Dic. Not I, by Heaven—not for the shield of him :
Nod he his plumes over the canteen bloaters.
If he gives tongue, I'll call the market clerks.
So I'll take up my goods and go within,
"To the music of my poultry's fluttering wings."

meant ' to get rid of a useless article in the quickest way one could.'   But
συκόφαντην is put παρὰ προσδοκίαν for σωρόν, as being fouler than any dust-
heap.   This passage has often been explained wrongly.   The Scholiasts
appear to have read—

> ἀλλ' ὦ ξένων βέλτιστε σὺ
> τοῦτον λαβὼν πρόσβαλλ' ὅποι, κ.τ.ἐ.

Chorus.

STROPHE.

There's a philosopher!   That's what is sensible!
    See what a number of good things he's got :
Some to a household complete indispensable,
    Others delicious to serve hot and hot.
All without trouble.   Ah, war is most odious,
    Ne'er in my home may I have such a pest;
Hateful were e'en the brave strain of Harmodius,
    Were I beside such unmannerly guest.
Yes, he's unmannerly ; how he broke in on us,
    Blest with prosperity's plenteous increase ;
Battle he brought, and confusion, and din on us,
    Turn'd a deaf ear to our offers of peace.
' Sit you,' we said, ' and to rest awhile deign with us.'
    Yet of his fires was our trellis the food ;
' Sit you beside us, the loving-cup drain with us.'
    Spilt of our vines was the costliest blood.

ANTISTROPHE.

Saw ye how proud he was ?   Now he's for jollity—
    Witness those feathers, how choice is his fare !
Beautiful playmate of Love and Frivolity,
    Little we knew, Peace, how lovely you were.
O that some Love-god would but bring me facing you,
    Love in the picture, with buds round his brows !
Old as I am, I should ne'er stop embracing you,
    Ne'er tire of kissing so buxom a spouse.

Then would I plant, for my mistress's pleasuring,[1]
    Many a sweet little vine-sprout a-row,
Rearing beside them, for motherly treasuring,
    Shoots of the fig-tree that tenderest blow.
Old as I am, yet no sprout should want cherishing ;
    Olivebranch-laden our farm should abound.
We should not dream of our cruise of oil perishing.
    We'd have enough for us all the year round.

The Herald *enters.*

Her. O yes, O yes ! Duly at sound of trump
Drink ; and whoever first has drained his flask
Shall get a skin as big as Ctesiphon's.
  Dic. What are ye doing, lads and wenches all ?
Did ye not hear the crier ? Braise, roast, turn,
Take the hare off the spit ; string on the wreaths ;
Hand me those skewers to truss the thrushes on.

Chor.	For your good sense I envy you,
	Still more for this first-rate *menu*,
	Of which you're boasting.
Dic.	You soon may say so, when you view
	My ducklings roasting.
Chor.	I think you're right.
Dic.	Rake out the grate.
Chor.	Saw you with·what an air of state
	(Or were you looking),
	Like some great *chef,* or *gourmet,* mate,
	He does his cooking ?

---

[1] The Coryphaeus figures Peace as his mistress. The result of their
union—their children—would be rural plenty, and all the arts of peace.

Peasant (*entering*). Ah, wretched me !

Dic.   Gods, who is this ?

Peas.   A man
In piteous case.

Dic.   Then keep it to yourself.

Peas. O sir, you've got the Peace ; measure me out
A little drop, if only for five years.

Dic. What ails you ?

Peas.   I'm a ruin'd man : I've lost
Both of my oxen.

Dic.   Whence ?

Peas.   From Phyle, sir,
Boeotians took them—

Dic.   Yet you're dressed in white.

Peas. That kept me, too, God knows, in every muck,
No—luck, I mean.

Dic.   Well, then, what want you now ?

Peas. I've cried my eyes out for those steers of mine.
So if you pity Dércetes of Phyle,
Anoint my eyelids with a drop of Peace.

Dic. But, my poor friend, I'm not the public leech.

Peas. Do, pray ; perhaps I might get back my oxen.

Dic. No, go to Pittalus' dispensary,
And blubber there.

Peas.   Just squeeze one drop into
This reed.

Dic.   No, not a cheep or twitter of it.
Go and be hang'd.

Peas.   Alas, my pair of steers !

Chor. He's found the sweets the treaty brings,
          Our friend ; and feels no generous stings
              To share and spoil them.

Dic. Pour honey o'er those chitterlings ;
          Those cuttles, broil them.
Chor. You hear his loud directions.
Dic.   Fry
          Those eels.
Chor.   You'll kill the passers-by
          And me ; you'll crush us
          Beneath that steam so savoury,
          Those words so luscious.
Dic. Now, roast them well, and brown them carefully.
Bridesman (entering). Ho, Dicaeopolis.
Dic.   Who's there ?
Brid.   This meat
The bridegroom sends you from his wedding feast.
Dic. And very kind of him, whoe'er he is.
Brid. And in return he wanted you to pour
A gill of peace into this gallipot,
So that he may not serve but stay at home.
Dic. Away with it.   Offer me not the meat.
I would not give it for a thousand drachmas.
But who is this ?
Brid.   The bridesmaid with a message
Sent by the bride, and only for your ears.
Dic. Well, what have *you* to say ?—Absurd, i'faith,
This bride's request, and urged most earnestly,
That she may keep at home her lord's—affections.
Bring me the Peace ; I'll give to her alone :
For she's a woman, nor deserves to taste
War's horrors.   Here, hold out your ointment-box,
And tell the bride that, when the lists are filling,
Her lord at night must use this embrocation.
Take back the Peace.   Bring me the ladle here,
I want to pour the wine into the flasks.

Chor. And who is this that, with wide eyes of fear,
Strides in, as with some fearful tidings charged ?
Messenger. O general Lamachus and lamentation.
Lam. Who round my brazen-bastion'd castle brawls ?
Mess. The generals bid you make a rapid move
This day, with all your plumes and plumps of spears ;
And then to watch the passes in the snow.
They've information that, about the feast
Of Flasks and Pots, Boeotian freebooters
Will make a raid on us.
Lam.   O generals
More numerous than kind, is it not hard :
I am not suffer'd e'en to keep the Feast ?
Dic. Warlike Achaeo-Lamachean host !
Lam. Alas, *you* have the laugh against me now.
Dic. What ? Would'st thou fight with four-wing'd Geryon ?
Lam. Alack, what tidings he has brought to me !
Dic. Hah ! now what message brings this knave to me ?
Mess. Ho, Dicaeopolis.
Dic.   What is't ?
Mess.   To dinner—
Quick, quick ; and bring your sweetmeat-case and flask.
The priest of Dionysus summons you,
So now make haste : you stay the banqueters :
There's nothing wanting but your company.
Couches and tables, cushions, coverlets,
Garlands, and scent, and bonbons, wenches, too,
And sponge-cakes, cheese-cakes, seed-cakes, honey-cakes ;
And dancing girls [1] that sing Harmodius's strain
Charmingly. But make haste.

---

[1] 1093. I read ὀρχηστρίδες ἐς τὸ ' φίλταθ' 'Αρμόδι' οὐ ' καλαί, ' dancing

Lam.   Ah, luckless me !

Dic. Well, but you chose your patroness, the dire
Gorgon ; shut up the house ; put in the viands.

Lam. Boy, bring me out the knapsack with my rations.

Dic. And bring me my confectionery-box.

Lam. Get me my thymy salt, and onions, boy.

Dic. My salmon-cutlets ! Onions make me sick.

Lam. Get me my sandwich made of bloaters stale.

Dic. Get me my *bonne bouche.* I will cook it here.

Lam. Bring hither, boy, the feathers from my casque.

Dic. And me the wood-pigeons and thrushes bring.

Lam. Lovely and white this ostrich feather is.

Dic. Lovely and brown is this wood-pigeon's flesh.

Lam. Cease, fellow, making merry with my armour.

Dic. Pray, fellow, do not eye my thrushes so.

Lam. Bring out the case that holds my triple plume.

Dic. And hand to me the dish that holds the hare.

Lam. Have, then, the moths been nibbling at my crest ?

Dic. Shall I begin my dinner with hare-pâté ?

Lam. Fellow, you 'll not address me, if you please.

---

girls famous for the Harmodius song,' which is here designated by its first
line, which ran—

φίλταθ' 'Αρμόδι' οὔ τί πω τέθνηκας.

These dancing girls, no doubt, sang as they danced, this popular Athenian
σκολιόν, to which allusion is made, sup. 980. The Scholiast there tells us
that the allusion is to the song of Harmodius, but such an allusion cannot
here be attained without changing the text. To explain ' pretty dancing
girls, the favourites of Harmodius,' is absurd. There is no reason to suppose that Harmodius was an admirer of dancing girls, and τὰ φίλταθ'
'Αρμοδίου could not mean 'such as H. would have loved.' The song is
designated by a few words of its first line, just as we would say, 'The heart
bow'd down,' or, ' The Harp that once,' or, ' Believe me, if all.' So

Dic. No ;—but we've been this long time arguing,
The slave and I. (*To the* Slave) Come, will you make a
  bet ?
And Lamachus, as umpire, will decide:
Locusts or thrushes—which the sweeter fare ?
Lam. You mock me, sir.
Dic.   Locusts, he says, by far.
Lam. Take down my spear, and bring it hither, boy.
Dic. Take off the chitterlings and bring them, boy.
Lam. Come, let me take the spear-case off my spear.
Take hold, boy.
Dic.   And you, boy, take hold of this.
Lam. Bring me the trestles that sustain my buckler.
Dic. And me the biscuits that sustain my stomach.
Lam. Bring me my buckler's dread-encircled round.
Dic. And me my pâté's cheese-encircled round.
Lam. Flat insolence is this for men to hear.
Dic. And excellent this cake for men to taste.
Lam. Pour oil, boy, on the shield. In it I see
An old man who'll be tried for shirking service.

Persius calls the Aeneid *Arma virum ;* and Cicero calls even his prose
treatises by the first words, referring to the *De Senectute* under the name
O Tite. As many words of the σκολιόν as will fit into the metre are used
to designate the song. Cicero, in a letter, thinks *Granius autem* enough
to indicate the maxim put into the mouth of Granius by Lucilius :—

Granius autem,
Non contemnere se et reges odisse superbos.

For καλὸς ἐς, 'good at a thing,' see L. S. under καλός II. The words
φίλταθ' 'Αρμόδι' οὔ τι πω τέθνηκας were the *beginning* of the σκολιόν. See
Schol. on 977 : ἐν ταῖς τῶν πότων συνόδοις ᾖδόν τι μέλος 'Αρμοδίου καλού-
μενον, οὗ ἡ ἀρχὴ, φίλτατε 'Αρμόδιε οὔ τι πω τέθνηκας. Cp. Ach. 1058,
Vesp. 1226 ; Lys. 633 ; Pelarg. Fr. 3.

E

Dic. Pour honey on the cake.   I see him here,
Telling Gorgasean Lamachus, go be hang'd.
   Lam. Boy, bring me out my breastplate for the fray.
   Dic. And bring me out my night-cap—that's the bowl.
   Lam. With this I'll fortify me 'gainst the foe.
   Dic. With this I'll fortify me for the fun.
   Lam. Boy, bind my kit securely to my shield.
   Dic. Boy, bind the viands safely on the tray.
   Lam. I'll take my knapsack up, and bear it off.
   Dic. And I will take my mantle up, and go.
   Lam. Take up my buckler, boy, and march therewith.
It snows.   Beshrew me !   'Tis a wintry scene.
   Dic. Take up the viands.   'Tis a festive scene.

Chorus.

(*To* Lamachus *and* Attendants).
Away then with joy to the field and the foe.
   (*To* Dicaeopolis *and* Lamachus.)
On what very dissimilar errands you go.
One to drink deep amid garlands of roses,
Stretch'd on the couch where young Beauty reposes.
   (*To* Lamachus.)
But you, a far different choice you have made,
To shiver in trenches and keep your parade.

Strophe.

Send, Zeus, on that blatant verse-mongering[1] Splutterer,
On Antimachus send the worse curse man could utter or

---

[1] For ξυγγραφῆ, which violates the metre, I suggest ζαγραφῆ, 'voluminous,'
a word not found, but formed on the analogy of ζαφλεγής, ζατρεφής. The
Scholiast tell us there was another Antimachus, who was a prose writer.
Hence arose the corrupt ξυγγραφῆ.

Think of. 'Twas he, that most niggardly beast,
When we won with the *Feasters* ne'er gave us our feast.
  May I gloat upon him starving
   For a plate of cuttle fish ;
  May he see it fit for carving,
   Cook'd and hissing on the dish
  ' By the salt ; ' [1] and then as up he
   Takes it, on his plate to land,
  May some little thievish puppy
   Snatch it from his very hand.

ANTISTROPHE.

And be this my first curse.   And the next may Night bring
  on him,
As he's trudging home, sick of parade, may there spring on
  him
Some tipsy rough, mad as Orestes of yore,
And fracture his skull ere he reaches his door.
  Stooping then a stone to snatch up,
   Wherewithal to lay him flat,
  In the darkness may he catch up
   Something not so hard as that.
  With this weapon arm'd completely,
   May he rush upon the foe,
  Miss his man, and, missing, featly
   Lay the daft Cratinus low.

      [Enter Servant of LAMACHUS.

---

[1] The Athenians' trireme, the Paralus, was always kept ready for sailing.
Hence it was always ' by the salt sea.' The cuttle fish, when dished for
dinner, would also be ' by the salt,' which would stand beside the plate for
use.

Serv. Ye vassals in the halls of Lamachus,
Heat ye, O heat ye water in a pot.
Make ready lint and salve, and greasy wool,
Charpie, and splint for dislocated bone.
For with a stake, in leaping o'er a trench,
Our hero's put his ankle out of joint,
And falling fractured on a stone his skull,
And has awaked the Gorgon from his shield.
And as the mighty puffinstrutter's plume
Fell on the crags, it shrill'd a grisly cry,
"Hail, glorious orb : farewell : I'm leaving now
What was my Dayspring, and I am no more."
Thus having said, he falls into a gutter,
Rises, and, rallying his runaways,
Smites the marauding ruffians hip and thigh.

    Lam.   Ah me ! for the spear
                Struck a terrible blow;
            But worse is the fear
                That vexes me so,
Lest that wretch Dicaeopolis see me, and laugh o'er my pitiful
    woe.

    Dic.   Dear me, but her breast
                Is as firm as a quince!
            Come, kiss me your best,
                O my sweet jewels, since
It was I drain'd the flask first and foremost, with never a wink
    or a wince.

    Lam. Alas, for all my miserable woes,
            And for my wound's sharp throes.

Dic. Good morrow to you, Lamachus, old chappie.

Lam.   Alack, my fate unhappy.

'26 *Dic. (speaking to the girl on his knee).* Wilt never to an end
     thy kisses bring ?

Lam.   I am a cursed thing.

Dic. Nor quench with fond caress thy hot desire ?

Lam.   Alas that charge so dire !

Dic. Show me the man that made a charge, I pray,
          On the Flasks' gala day.

Lam. O Paean, healing god, on thee I call.

Dic.   'Tis not his festival.

Lam. Take hold, take hold, my gentle friends, I beg,
          And firmly grasp my leg.

Dic. And around me, sweet girls, your soft arms fling,
          And, closely kissing, cling.

Lam. My head is dizzy with its grievous pain,
          And reels my weary brain.

Dic. My thoughts run wild on love's luxurious bed,
          And paths of dalliance tread.

Lam. Lend healing hands and bear me, I beseech,
          To Pittalus, the leech.

Dic. Off to the judges : is the King within ?
          Yield me the victor's skin.

Lam. This horrid spear is piercing me ; thro' flesh and
          bone it's driven.

Dic. Huzza ! I've emptied it. Huzza ! my cheers shall
          rend the Heaven.

Chor. Huzza, then, since you challenge me ; your
          victory is glorious.

Dic.   I fill'd a bumper neat, and then without a wink I
          drain'd it.

Chor. Huzza, my hearty.   Now take off the wineskin, for
          you've gain'd it.

Dic.   Sing ' Lo the conquering hero comes.'   Huzza,
          I am victorious !

Chor.   Well, we'll attend you to your door,
                And tell your triumph's story ;
             And shout hip, hip, hurrah before
                We leave you with your glory.

THE END.

www.ingramcontent.com/pod-product-compliance
Lightning Source LLC
Chambersburg PA
CBHW020241090426
42735CB00010B/1784